Picturesque
NORFOLK

painted by A. Heaton Cooper
and other artists

POPPYLAND NEAR SHERINGHAM
by Annie L. Pressland

SALMON

Published by
J Salmon Limited
100 London Road, Sevenoaks,
Kent TN13 1BB

Designed by the Salmon Studio

Copyright © 1995 J Salmon Limited

ISBN 1 898435 28 6

Printed in England by
J Salmon Limited, Tubs Hill Works
Sevenoaks, Kent

Custom House, Lynn.

Coloured Illustrations

WROXHAM BRIDGE - A RAINY DAY
by A. Heaton Cooper

Acle Bridge.

AROUND BROADLAND

The Broadland waters cover an area of over 3000 acres of which the largest, Breydon Water, occupies about a third and, with the river valleys of which they form part, produce a type of scenery unique in Great Britain. Though Broadland is irremedially flat, and in many parts so utterly featureless that the drainage mills are the only objects that break the monotony of the landscape, yet Nature is generous in her compensations and the atmospheric effects are so marvellous as to more than atone for the abscence of scenic grandeur. Those who have once come under the spell of Broadland return year after year to the rivers and marshes.

For sailing purposes the Waveney and Yare have many advantages but the most varied and attractive scenery is to be found on the Bure between Acle and Coltishall, and on its tributaries the Thurne and Ant. Mile after mile of river and broad is bounded by tall reeds, or lines of pollarded willows, with flat green pastures stretching as far as the eye can see, the vista broken only by the sails of some passing yacht, the windmills that once drained the marshes, the tower of a distant church on the bordering ridges, a few reed-thatched cottages or an ancient inn. Broadland has many distinctive features, none more so than the white sailed drainage mills which once dominated the landscape but now are sadly a rarity. Also characteristic is the Norfolk wherry, long low boats, probably Dutch in

On the Bure.

origin, which carry an enormous sail and draw very little water. Now confined to a few boats the wherries once dominated river traffic. Some were large, up to 80 tons, the trading wherries with just a cabin at the stern, whilst the pleasure wherries were all cabin.

The Norfolk Broads are a naturalists paradise and are renowned for their particular abundance of birdlife. One of the most beautiful of the Broadland birds is the bearded tit. Although it is possible to be a frequent visitor to the waterways without either hearing or seeing one, nevertheless at the right time these agile birds may be seen running up the reeds or with a dipping flight crossing one of the little bays on the margins of certain broads. Another striking bird is the great-crested grebe whose remarkable diving powers are frequently demonstrated. The heron is conspicuous from its size,

Potter Heigham Bridge.

whether slowly winging its way to or from the heronry, or standing thigh deep in the water waiting patiently for fish. Coots are very abundant on some of the broads, and moorhens in the fringe of vegetation along most of the streams. The bittern is now sparingly distributed in East Norfolk but its marvellous 'boom' is still one of the most astonishing Broadland sounds during the nesting season.

AN EEL-FISHER ON THE BURE
by A. Heaton Cooper

HORNING FERRY ON THE BURE
by A. Heaton Cooper

IRSTEAD CHURCH BY THE ANT
by A. Heaton Cooper

BARTON BROAD
by A. Heaton Cooper

WINDMILLS ON THE THURNE
by A. Heaton Cooper

HICKLING BROAD
by A. Heaton Cooper

HEIGHAM SOUND - THUNDER CLOUDS
by A. Heaton Cooper

EEL'S FOOT INN, ORMESBY
by A. Heaton Cooper

NORWICH FROM MOUSEHOLD HEATH
by A. Heaton Cooper

The Castle, Norwich.

NORWICH – A FINE CITY

Norwich has been called a 'city of gardens', a 'city of churches' and a 'city of bridges' and all of these are applicable. This is its charm – here the past unites with the present. Some of the older city streets contain hardly a modern building; in others the tall gables of the plaster houses, or the more substantial residences of faced flint, mingle happily with structures of more recent date.

Much of quaint old Norwich centres around the cathedral close. Remains of the old watergate are to be found at Pull's Ferry, and of the other gateways, the Erpingham Gate, which gives access to picturesque Tombland, was erected about 1420 and the Ethelbert Gate about 1275. Norwich Cathedral, with its graceful 315 feet high spire, is, after Durham, the most complete Norman cathedral throughout all England, being consecrated in 1101. Of the exterior the magnificent east end, with its flying buttresses, is the most striking feature, whilst the interior is notable for the massive Norman pillars and fine roof – the nave vault contains 328 carved

Tombland, Norwich.

bosses depicting Scriptural scenes.

Relics of the walls which enclosed the medieval town can still be seen at Norwich. The length of the wall on the south side of the Wensum was one and a half miles, and on the north side three-quarters of a mile, the boundary being completed by two sections of the river, so that the entire circuit of the city would have been some

Erpingham Gate, Norwich.

four miles. Originally the walls were twenty feet high and over three feet thick, and ,although all the gates have been pulled down, there are remains of several towers, including the brick-built Cow Tower, situated on the south bank of the Wensum. The Norman castle, with its massive ninety feet square keep, is also well preserved and very striking.

DAWN PATROL - WIGEON MOVING OUT TO SEA
by Roland Green MBOU, FRSA

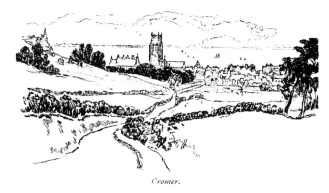

Cromer.

THE NORTH NORFOLK COAST

Beyond Mundesley the cliffs rise to their greatest height around Cromer. Much of the scenery of north-east Norfolk is wooded and the views from Beacon Hill and Pretty Corner provide a wide diversity of hill and dale, sea and woodland. Cromer and Sheringham are two of the fishing villages which have developed into popular resorts. Both owe their attraction as much to the beauty of their surroundings – for many miles along this stretch of coast the cliff walks provide delightful vistas not only of sea and sand, but of the wooded heights inland.

The landward side of the beach from Sheringham westward to Blakeney Point ten miles away is formed by a ridge of pebbles; protected by this huge shingle bank is an extensive range of tidal marshes traversed by creeks. Beyond Kelling the coast road borders the marshes below the wild expanse of Salthouse Heath towards Cley-next-the-Sea, where the main street is narrow and winding and bears evidence of the days when Cley was a seaport. The striking windmill forms a picturesque scene which has been perpetuated by many artists. Blakeney, its narrow street winding down the hill from the church to the quay, was once the foremost port along the coast and sent ships to fight the Spanish Armada. The church of St Nicholas occupies one of the most commanding positions in the county – the tower is 104 feet high and at the north-east angle of the church is a slender turret said to have been

Abbey Gateway, Walsingham.

used as a beacon to guide sailors. The harbour contains some five square miles of water at high tide and Blakeney Point forms one of the finest nature reserves in the country. It has long been famous for its birdlife, both residents and the spring and autumn migrants.

Beyond Blakeney is the isolated village of Morston, and Stiffkey, clustering alongside a little stream in a valley between the chalk hills; it is noted for its cockles, the famous "Stewkey Blues". Wells-next-the-Sea is a small seaport with a picturesque quay and harbour – a steep, straight embankment runs from the town to the beach. Inland lies the little priory town of Walsingham, probably as unaffected by the hand of time as any. A ramble through the quiet streets will reveal domestic architecture of the past five or six centuries and close by is distinctive East Barsham Manor, a

East Barsham Manor House.

wonderful example of ornamental brickwork.

West of Wells the Holkham sand dunes have largely been planted with trees and the salt marshes were enclosed and banked in the 18th century. The magnificent mansion of Holkham Hall stands within a park nine miles in circumference. Burnham Overy Staithe is a pretty little place which presents a colourful boating scene. Here the 'Norfolk Hero', Lord Nelson, learned to sail - his father was rector of Burnham Thorpe, a little way inland.

THE COAST ROAD, SALTHOUSE
by Martin Hardie RWS

THE MILL, CLEY-NEXT-THE-SEA
by Martin Hardie RWS

COTTAGES AT CLEY-NEXT-THE-SEA
By J.C.T. Willis RI

THE CREEK, BLAKENEY
by Martin Hardie RWS

THE QUAY, BLAKENEY
by J.C.T. Willis RI

MORSTON CHURCH
by Martin Hardie RWS

THE QUAY, WELLS-NEXT-THE-SEA
by A. Heaton Cooper

BURNHAM OVERY STAITHE
by Martin Hardie RWS

THE SOUTH GATE, KING'S LYNN
by A. Heaton Cooper

Lynn from the River.

WEST NORFOLK

Norfolk is unique among the counties of the East Coast in having a shoreline which faces west; between Hunstanton and King's Lynn the coast follows the fringes of The Wash. To the north of Hunstanton are perhaps the wildest and loneliest stretches, around the sandhills where Holme bounds Thornham; desolate dunes with wiry marram grass, creeks and drains filled by every flood tide and mile after mile of salt marsh richly coloured with the beautiful mauve blossoms of sea lavender.

New Hunstanton owes its fine position to the fact that the chalk downs here meet the sea, and there is about a mile of cliff providing a charming study in rock formations and colours. From the old lighthouse the cliff slopes southwards to the sandhills of Heacham and northwards to Old Hunstanton. Here the village has the charm which the mellowing hand of time alone can give; old walls of brick, chalk and flint, with patches of red valerian, the pond, the

The Town Hall, Lynn.

magnificent trees, the spacious and well-kept churchyard, form a fitting setting for the beautiful church.

King's Lynn is noted for its fine merchants' houses and impressive Custom House, a survival of the time when, as Defoe said in 1722, it had "the greatest extent of inland navigation of any port in England, London excepted". It remains one of the finest examples of a prosperous seafaring town, much of its domestic architecture untouched by the passage of time and reflecting the Low Countries

Houghton Hall and Church

influence which pervades much of the East Coast. Prominent are the lofty Greyfriars Tower and the grand Church of St Margaret, founded in 1101.

From King's Lynn excursions can be made to Castle Rising, with its stout stone keep, to Sandringham, country residence of the Royal Family and to Houghton Hall, the Palladian mansion built for Robert Walpole, the first Prime Minister.

THE KEEP, CASTLE RISING
by A. Heaton Cooper

SANDRINGHAM HOUSE
by A. Heaton Cooper

THE HERRING HARVEST, GREAT YARMOUTH
by A. Heaton Cooper

The Quay, Yarmouth.

AROUND GREAT YARMOUTH

Old views of Yarmouth show the town mainly as a series of windmills and lookouts for fishermen, but the opening of the fish wharf by the river in 1868 and the consequent removal of the fishing industry from the beach, and the development of the town as a popular seaside resort, entirely changed its character. The narrow 'rows' still remain one of its remarkable features. At one time there were 145 of them with a total length of seven miles. When the skippers and fishermen all lived in the rows, watchmen were employed to go up and down them to "cry the wind". For many years Yarmouth was the principal herring fishing port in the British Isles, and the largest catch ever brought into the town on one day was the 72 million fish landed on 23rd October, 1907. 'Yarmouth Bloaters' – a prized delicacy – are herrings traditionally caught between the months of October and December, slightly salted and oak-smoked.

Yarmouth Beach.

Yarmouth's history dates back to 1260 when a charter was granted empowering the inhabitants to fortify the town with a wall and a moat. The most impressive ancient building in the town is St Nicholas's Church, the largest parish church in England; it encompasses 23,000 square feet in area and is wider than York Minster.

To the south of Yarmouth is Gorleston-on-Sea, at the mouth of the River Yare. It is a combination of past and present, with a harbour

Caister Castle

and fine beaches. Gorleston was a minor Roman outpost when the land on which Yarmouth now stands was still buried beneath the sea. On a coast where the effects of erosion have been most severely felt Yarmouth is the exception for here the sea receded over the centuries. Beyond Yarmouth is Caister, with its picturesque ruined castle, built by Sir John Falstaff in the middle of the 15th century, and then California where the sea is approached by a 'gap'. The 'scores' of the Suffolk coast and the 'gaps' of the Norfolk coast were probably formed by subterranean springs which undermined the cliffs.

EAST DEREHAM
by A. Heaton Cooper

Horsham St. Faith's.

MID NORFOLK

Inland Norfolk is full of interest with delightful country towns and villages, ancient castles and monastic ruins and fine stately homes. The principal centres are the towns of East Dereham, Swaffham and Wymondham, the latter noted for their fine market crosses. The cross at Swaffham, within the town's particularly extensive market square, was built in 1783 at a cost of £400, half of which was spent on the statue of Ceres which surmounts the leaded dome. The old market cross at Wymondham was destroyed by fire in 1615, and the present one, a well preserved structure of wood and plaster was erected three years later. It is octagonal, resting on wooden pillars with stone bases. The town is dominated by the massive Abbey Church, founded in 1107. East Dereham also has a fine flint church, the second largest in Norfolk. Near the tower are pretty Bishop Bonner's Cottages, named after a former rector who once owned them.

As well as the fine churches there are numerous other ecclesiastical

Blickling Hall.

remains of note, of which probably the most graceful are the Priory ruins at Castle Acre . A Cluniac foundation, dating from 1089, the West Front is especially impressive and a glorious example of Norman work, filled with arches and columns. Close by are the massive earthworks of the Norman castle.

For exploring the hinterland of north-east Norfolk the neighbouring towns of Aylsham and North Walsham, also with a colonnaded market cross dating from the 16th century, are well placed. Near

Wymondham Market Cross.

Aylsham is magnificent Blickling Hall, a red-brick quadrangular building with oriel windows and an ornamented porch, begun by Sir John Hobart in 1620, one of many Norfolk houses notable for their fine brickwork; another excellent Tudor example is Oxburgh Hall, near Swaffham, a castellated building, with an 80 feet high gatehouse, all surrounded by a wide moat.

SWAFFHAM MARKET PLACE
by A. Heaton Cooper

THE PRIORY RUINS, CASTLE ACRE
by A. Heaton Cooper

THE MARKET CROSS, NORTH WALSHAM
by A. Heaton Cooper